PLANET JUPITER

By Emily Kington

CONTENTS

First published in 2026 by Hungry Tomato Ltd
F15, Old Bakery Studios, Blewetts Wharf, Malpas Road,
Truro, Cornwall, TR1 1QH, UK.

A CIP catalog record for this book is available from the British Library.

ISBN 9781835696804

Manufactured in the USA

Discover more at
www.hungrytomato.com

Front cover image is an artist's impression of Jupiter as seen from the surface of one of its moons. Title page image is an edited image of Jupiter. Contents page image is an edited image of Jupiter.

Words in **BOLD** can be found in the glossary.

WHERE IS JUPITER?

Jupiter

Sun

There are eight planets in our **solar system**. The planets travel around the Sun. Jupiter is the fifth planet from the Sun.

The time it takes a planet to travel once around the Sun is called a year. Jupiter travels around the Sun once every 12 **Earth years**. This journey is called an **orbit**.

PLANET FACTS

Jupiter is the largest planet in our solar system. 1,000 Earths could fit inside it!

A day is the time it takes a planet to spin around once. Jupiter is the fastest spinning planet, with a day lasting just under 10 hours!

Jupiter is a **gas giant**. Scientists originally thought its **core** was solid, but **NASA**'s Juno spacecraft found information that suggests it might not be!

WHAT'S THE WEATHER LIKE?

Jupiter's quick spinning speed makes it a very stormy planet.

On Jupiter winds can reach up to 335 miles per hour (539 kilometers per hour), and storms can last for hundreds of years.

The Great Red Spot

The Great Red Spot is a huge storm that has been raging on Jupiter for 300 years. It is 15,400 miles (24,780 kilometers) wide, making it twice the size of Earth!

MOONS AND RINGS

Jupiter has four large **moons** and many smaller ones – 95 in total.

It makes Jupiter like a mini solar system all of its own!

Jupiter also has rings made of dust. These may have been created when **meteoroids** smashed into the moons closest to the planet.

Jupiter's rings

JUPITER'S MOONS

Scientists have used **probes** to study Jupiter's four largest moons.

Io is covered with the most active volcanoes in the solar system. Its surface is always changing.

Scientists think that there may be a liquid ocean beneath the frozen surface of Europa.

Europa

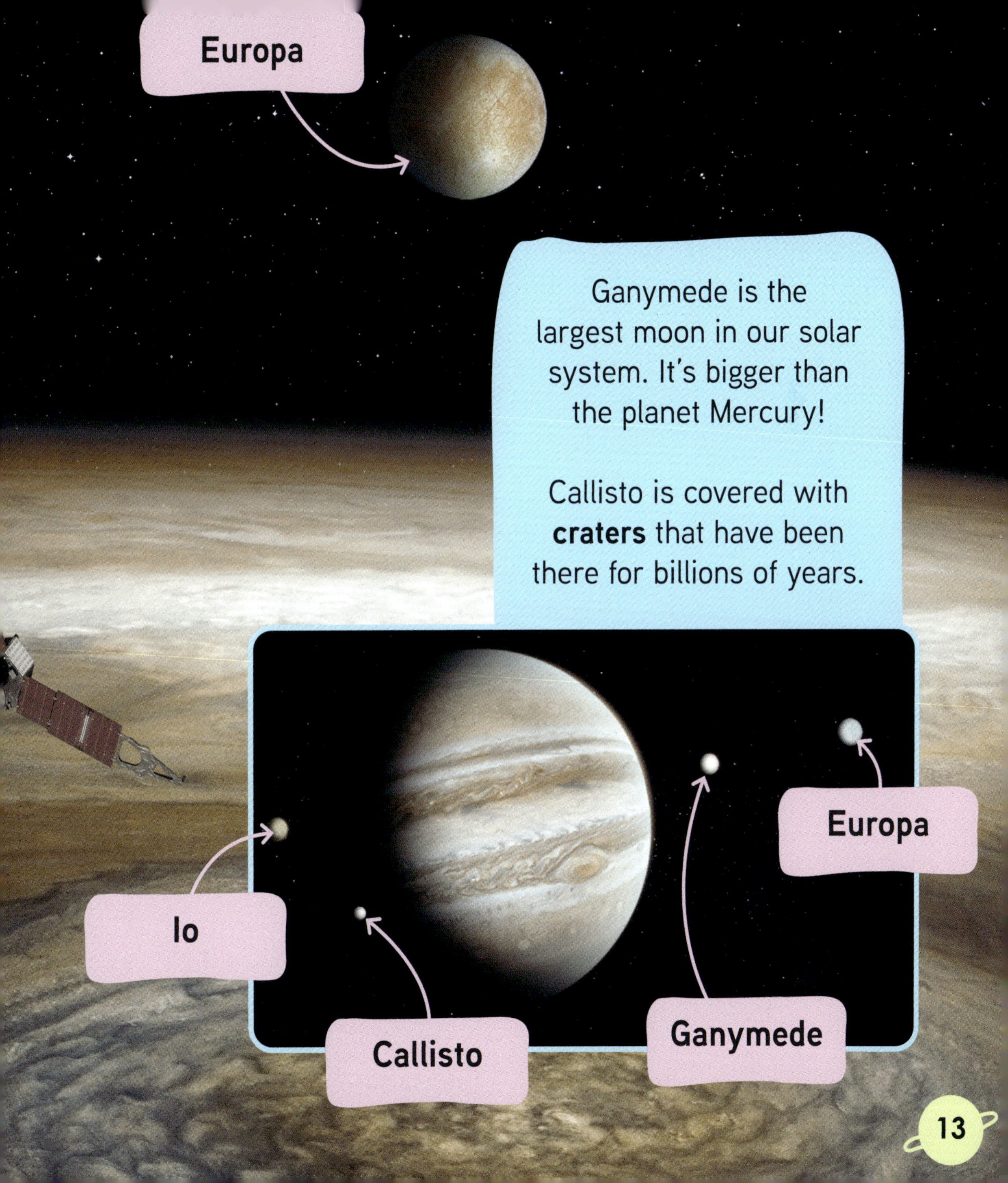

Ganymede is the largest moon in our solar system. It's bigger than the planet Mercury!

Callisto is covered with **craters** that have been there for billions of years.

FACT FILE

In Ancient Rome, **astronomers** could see Jupiter shining brightly in the night sky even without using **telescopes**.

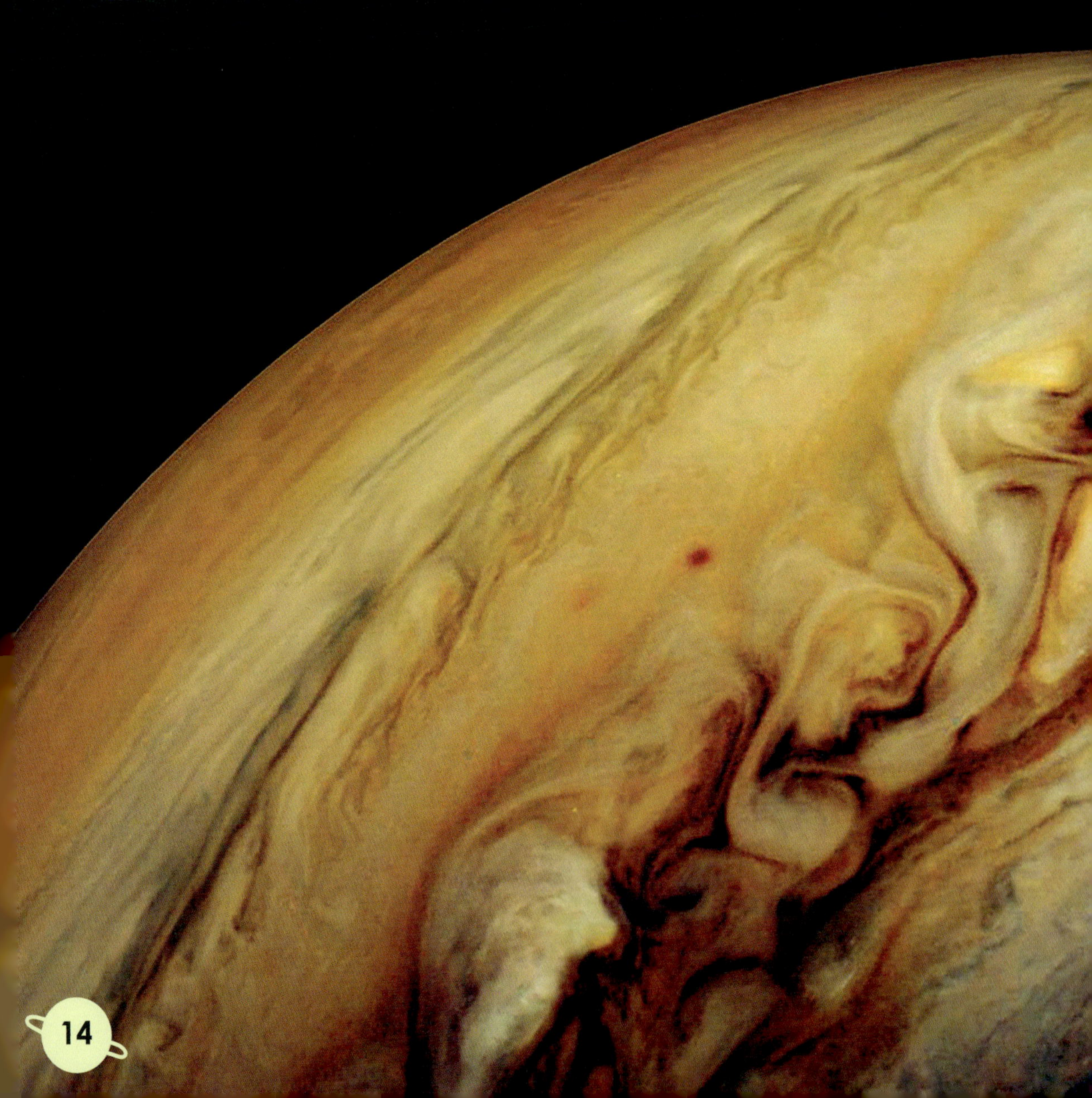

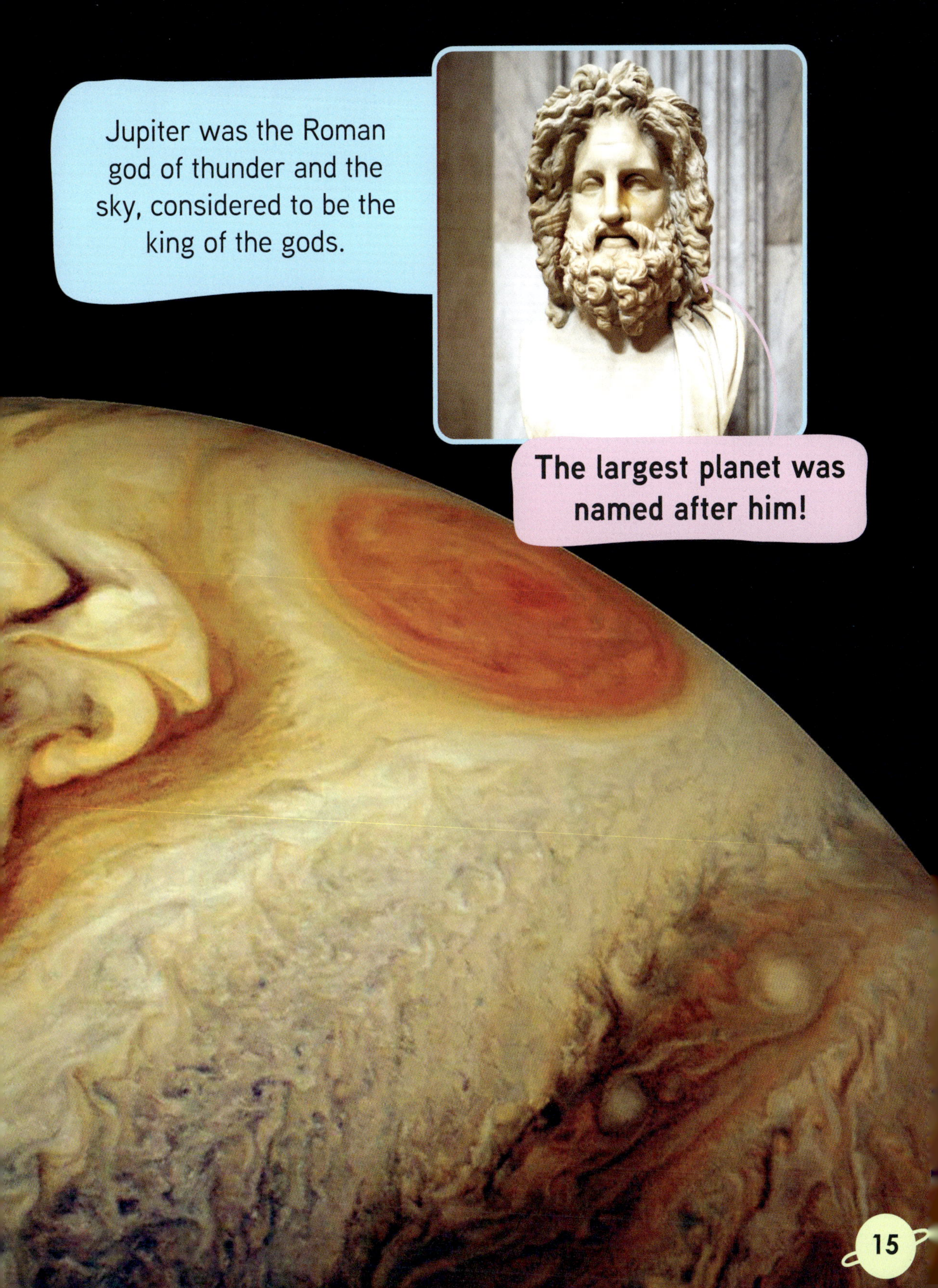
Jupiter was the Roman god of thunder and the sky, considered to be the king of the gods.
The largest planet was named after him!

WHAT CAN WE SEE?

From Earth on a clear night, you can see Jupiter in the sky using just your eyes.

With a small telescope it is also possible to see Jupiter's moons.

The **Hubble Space Telescope** that is in orbit around Earth is able to take clear photos of Jupiter.

Hubble Space Telescope

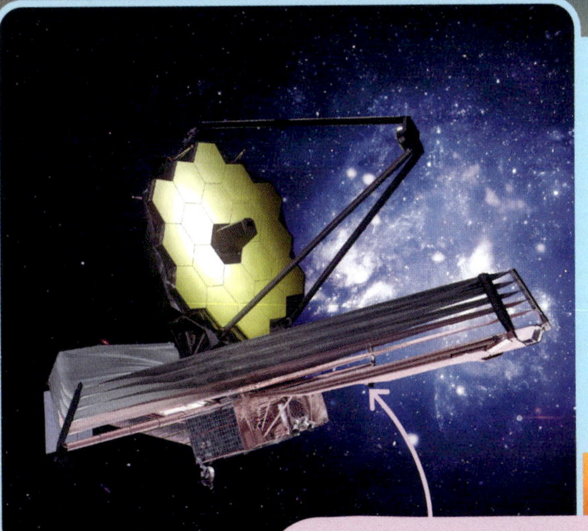

NASA's powerful **James Webb Space Telescope** orbits the Sun rather than Earth. It has taken amazing images of Jupiter that show it in incredible detail!

James Webb Space Telescope

MISSIONS TO JUPITER

While no human has ever traveled as far as Jupiter, many space probes have! It takes up to six years to travel there.

Pioneer 10 was the first mission to Jupiter and took the first close-up photographs of the planet.

Since NASA's Juno spacecraft arrived in 2016, its close **flybys** have given scientists lots of data to help them answer questions that they have been asking for years.

LOOKING FOR LIFE

Jupiter has a very thick **atmosphere**, no solid surface, and no water.

Jupiter's Surface

Because life as we know it needs water, scientists are not looking for life on Jupiter itself.

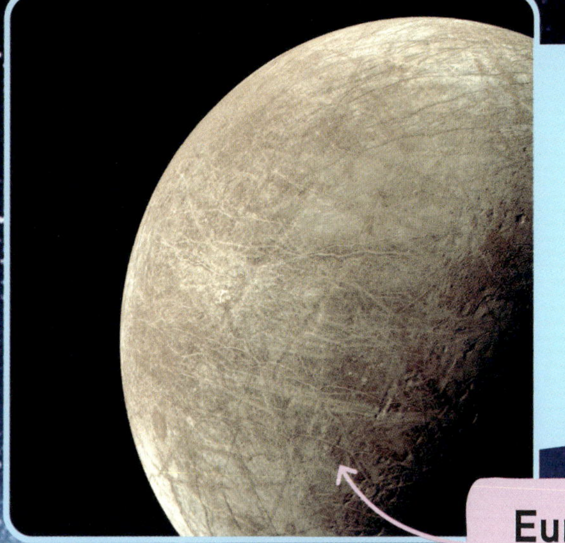

Scientists are much more excited by Jupiter's moon Europa, which they think has water under its outer layer. There could be twice as much water on Europa as there is on Earth!

Europa

The James Webb Space Telescope also found traces of **carbon dioxide** on Europa, which is another building block needed for life!

WHAT'S NEXT?

NASA's Europa Clipper probe was launched in October 2024.

Its mission is to see if Europa has conditions suitable for life.

It will collect data about its atmosphere and possible ocean, and will look for areas on its surface where future missions might land!

Europa Clipper

GLOSSARY

Astronomers – scientists who study space.

Atmosphere – the gases that surround a planet.

Carbon dioxide – an invisible gas in the air.

Core – the middle of a planet.

Craters – large holes that have been created by something hitting the ground.

Earth year – the amount of time that a year lasts for on Earth (365 days).

Flyby – the closest approach of a spacecraft to a planet or moon.

Gas – a substance that is neither solid or liquid and has no fixed shape. Many gases are invisible.

Gas giant – a large planet made of gas. Saturn and Jupiter are both gas giants.

Hubble Space Telescope – a telescope in orbit around Earth.

Hydrogen – a colorless, tasteless gas.

James Webb Space Telescope – a telescope in orbit around the Sun.

Meteoroid – small natural objects, such as rocks or metals, that travel through outer space.

Moons – large, natural objects that orbit a planet.

NASA – the National Aeronautics and Space Administration is an agency that deals with space exploration.

Orbit – the path taken by one object circling around another object in space.

Probes – spacecraft sent to explore outer space.

Solar system – the Sun and everything that moves around it.

Telescopes – instruments that make faraway objects appear bigger.

Picture credits:
(t=top; b=bottom; m=middle; l=left; r=right):

NASA: images-assets.nasa.gov/image/ARC-1972-AC72-2139/ARC-1972-AC72-2139~orig.jpg 18m; images-assets.nasa.gov/image/KSC-20241014-PH-SPX01_0002/KSC-20241014-PH-SPX01_0002~orig.jpg 22-23bg; images-assets.nasa.gov/image/PIA13920/PIA13920~orig.jpg 18bl; images-assets.nasa.gov/image/PIA21985/PIA21985~orig.jpg 9br; images-assets.nasa.gov/image/PIA22687/PIA22687~orig.jpg 8-9bg; images-assets.nasa.gov/image/PIA24321/PIA24321~orig.jpg 23tr; images-assets.nasa.gov/image/PIA24962/PIA24962~orig.jpg 14-15bg. Wikipedia: By Biser Todorov - Own work, CC BY 4.0 16tr. Shutterstock: Alones 18-19bg; Angela Cini 7br; Artsiom P 10ml, 24bg; AstroStar 16-17br; Claudio Caridl 21tl; Dima Zel 2-3bg, 17tr, 17ml; Eugenly Jamort 21mr; ManuMata 11tl; Mouhamed amin 13br; Mr.Sun.Three 20-21bg; Muratart 12-13bg; NASA Images 1bg; Triff 4-5bg; Vadim Sadovski 10-11bg; Whitelion61 6-7bg; Will Hilton-Kent 12m.